For the reader, with hope that you find joy within these pages – M.C

For my family and all the children who sing and move and love
and belong in their wonderful skin – M.S

First published in the United Kingdom in 2023 by Lantana Publishing Ltd.
Clavier House, 21 Fifth Road, Newbury RG14 6DN, UK
www.lantanapublishing.com | info@lantanapublishing.com

American edition published in 2023 by Lantana Publishing Ltd., UK.

Distributed in the United States and Canada by Lerner Publishing Group, Inc.
241 First Avenue North, Minneapolis, MN 55401, U.S.A.
For reading levels and more information, look for this title at www.lernerbooks.com.
Cataloging-in-Publication Data Available.

Hardback ISBN: 978-1-915244-54-3
eBook PDF ISBN: 978-1-915244-55-0
ePub3 ISBN: 978-1-915244-56-7

Printed and bound in China using sustainably sourced paper and plant-based inks.
Original artwork created digitally.

IN MY SKIN

MORGAN CHRISTIE
MARTINA STUHLBERGER

Lantana

In my skin, I **SING**.

My voice flows like a river running upstream.

I fill the world with my song.

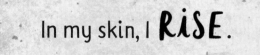

In my skin, I **RiSE.**

I climb as high as the mountain peaks.

I stand up and face challenges, whenever they come.

In my skin, I **REACH**.

I grow like the long curving limbs
of an oak tree.

I try my best at everything I do.

In my skin, I **MOVE**.

I spin like crinkly leaves on a windy day.

I dance to my very own rhythm.

In my skin, I **THiNK**.

My thoughts turn like the crisp pages
of the books we explore together.

I learn and let new ideas open up inside me.

In my skin, I **HOPE**.

I dust myself off so I can
take on tomorrow.

I chase the rainbow that shines after the storm.

In my skin, I **LAUGH**.

I can feel my smile stretching
from ear to ear.

My laughter rings
around the playground

for everyone to hear.

In my skin, I **REST**.

I am as quiet as the moon's gentle glow.

I breathe in and out, deep and calm.

In my skin, I **REMEMBER**.

I echo the songs passed down through generations.

I am the dream my ancestors dreamed.

In my skin, I **LOVE**.

My heart twirls like twisting roots that burrow into the earth.

I hug my loved ones tight and kiss them goodnight.

REST

HOPE

THINK

RISE

REACH

In my skin, I . . .

In my skin, I

BELONG.